Made in the USA
Coppell, TX
13 February 2020

15801847R00049